IF YOU CAN DRAW THESE THINGS →
YOU WILL BE ABLE TO DRAW
ALL THE THINGS IN THIS BOOK.

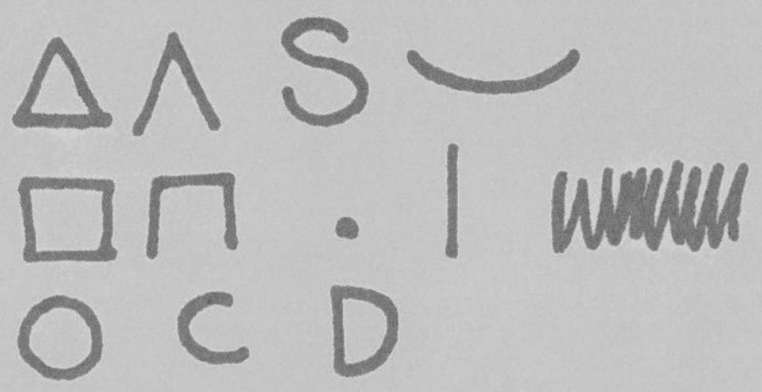

FOR INSTANCE —

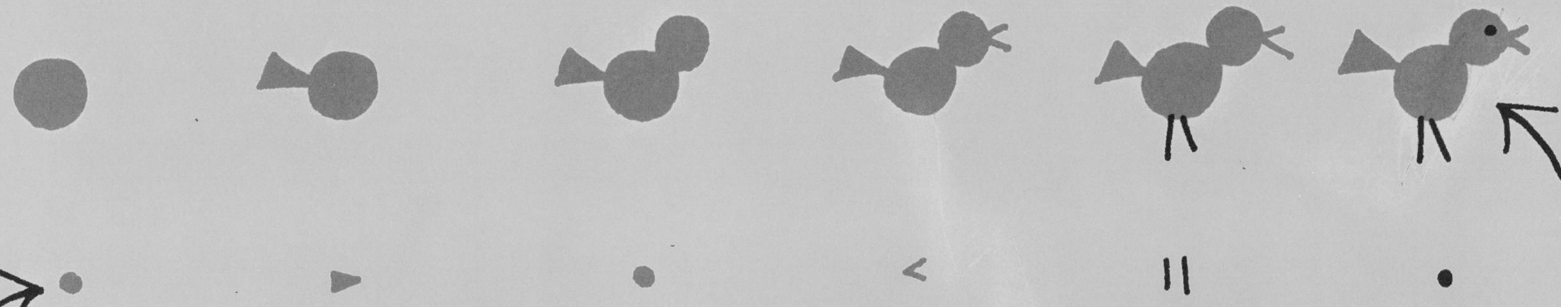

THE BOTTOM ROW TELLS WHAT TO DRAW | THE TOP ROW TELLS WHERE TO PUT IT.

VAMPIRE

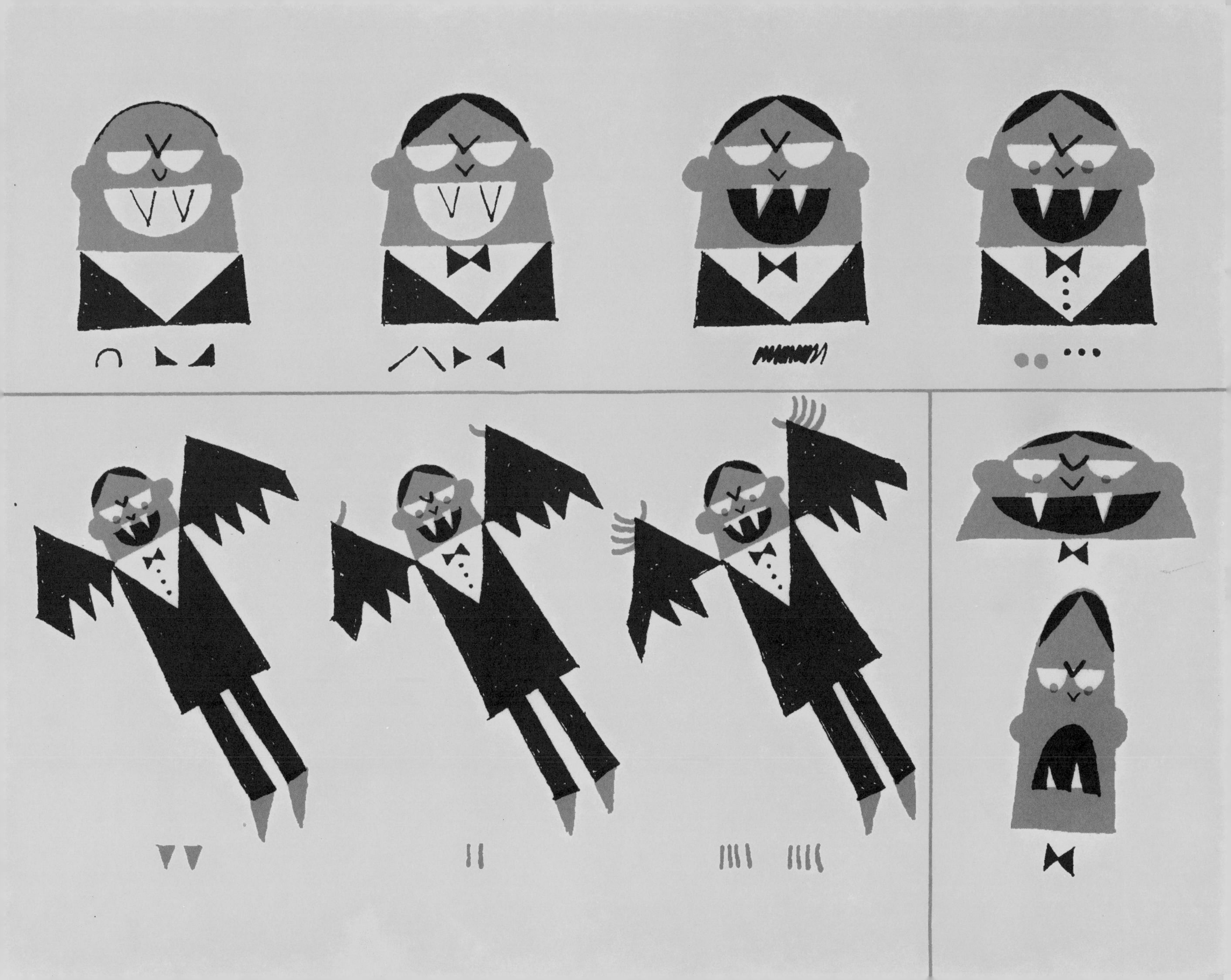

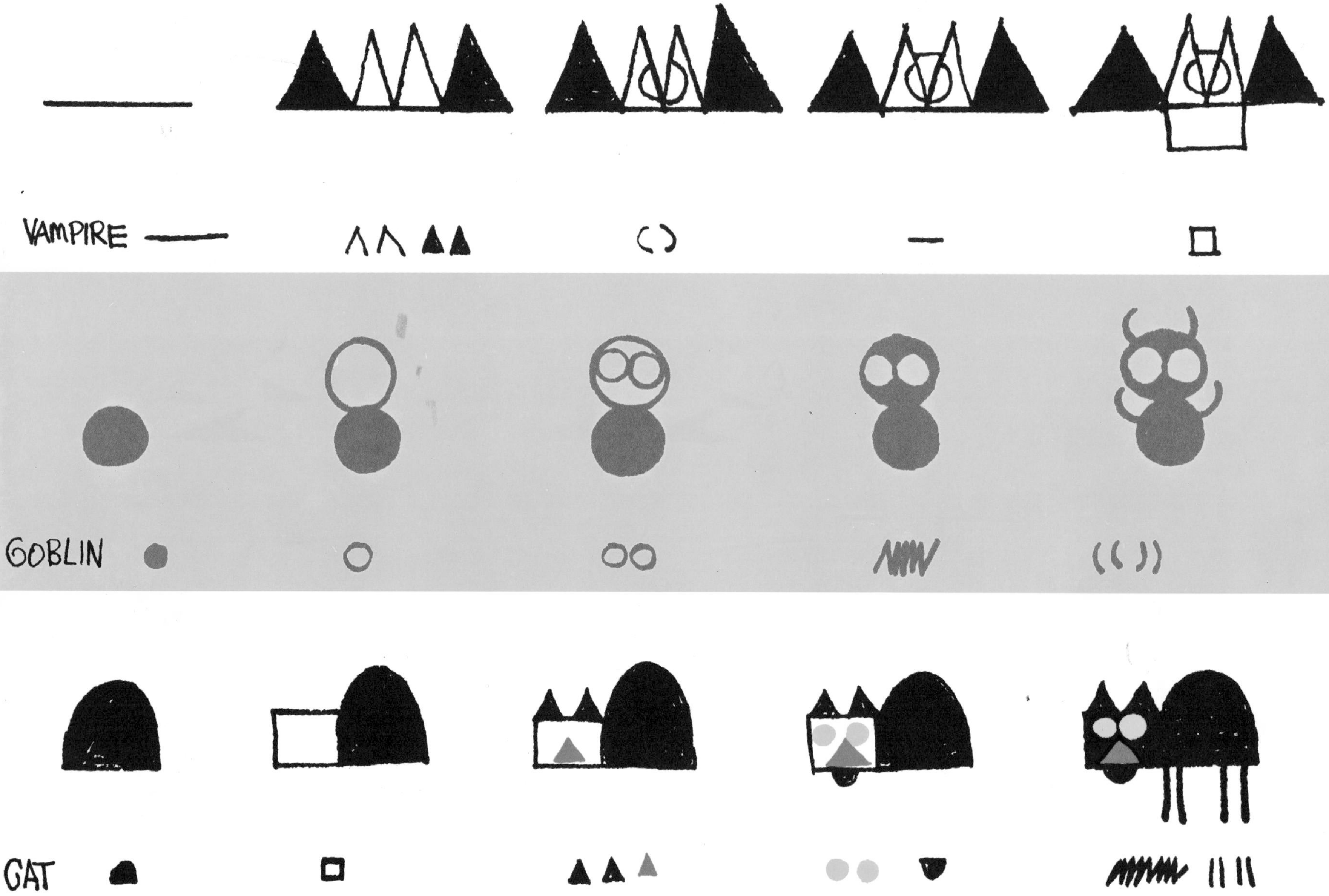
VAMPIRE
GOBLIN
CAT

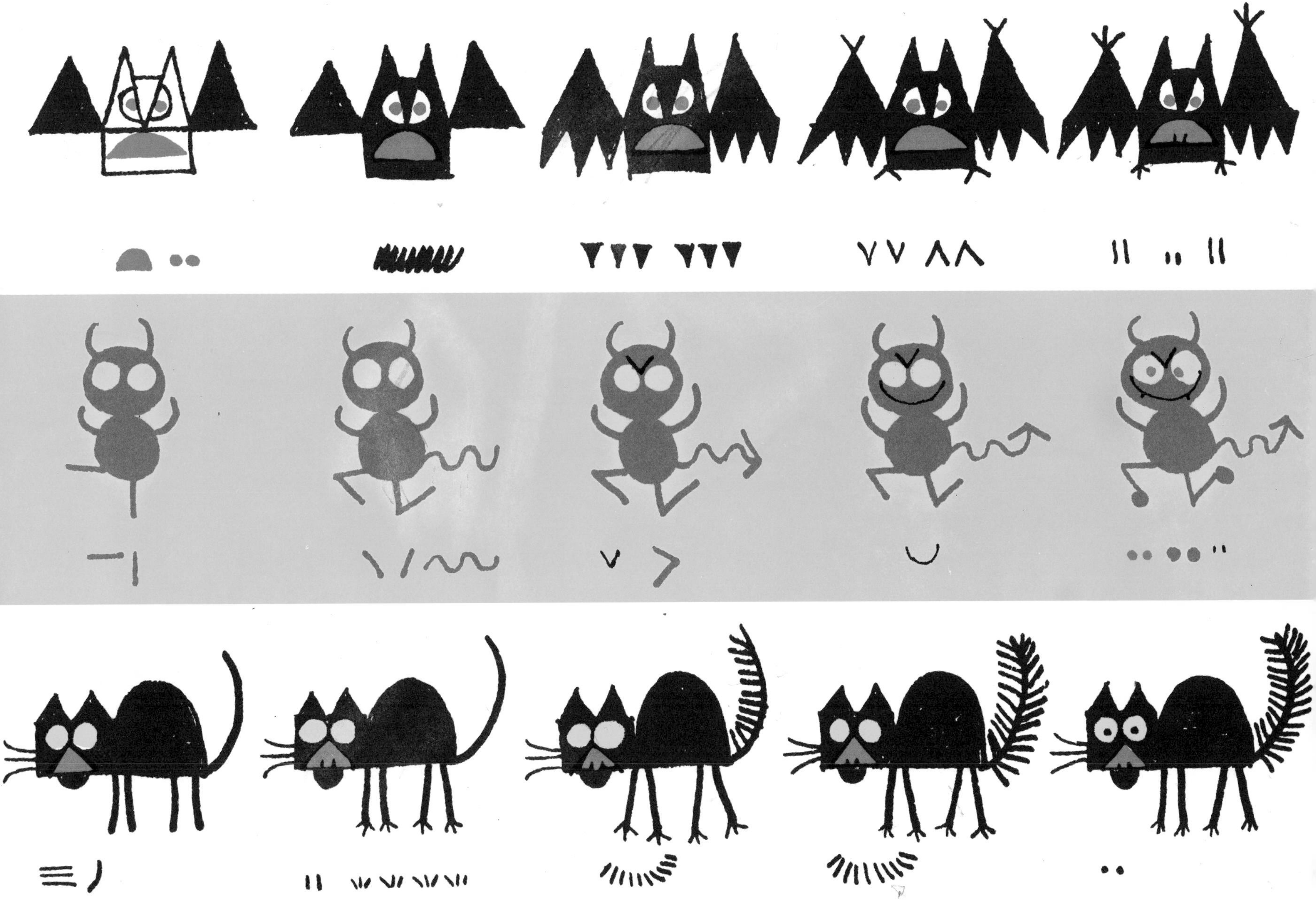

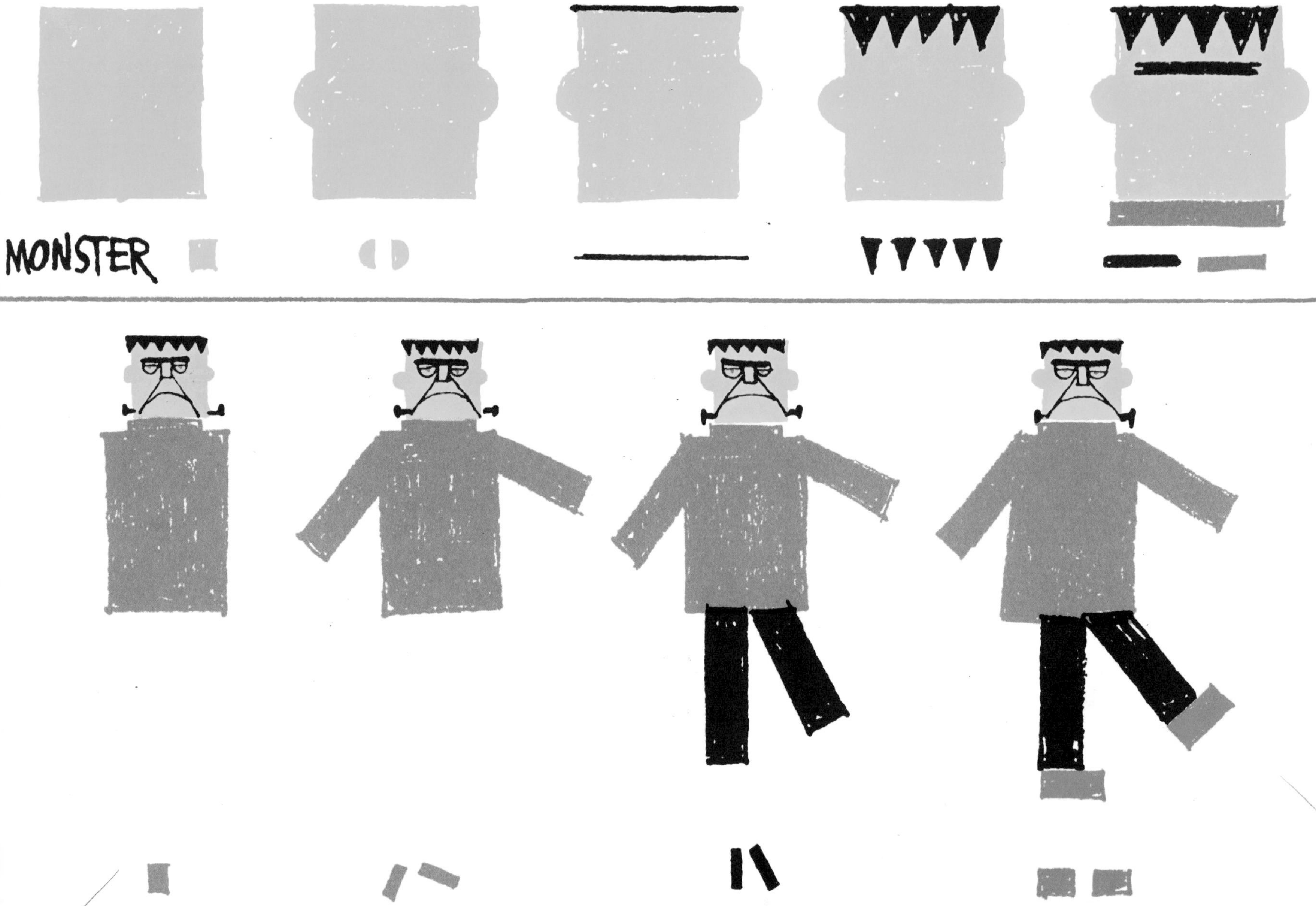
MONSTER

WITCH

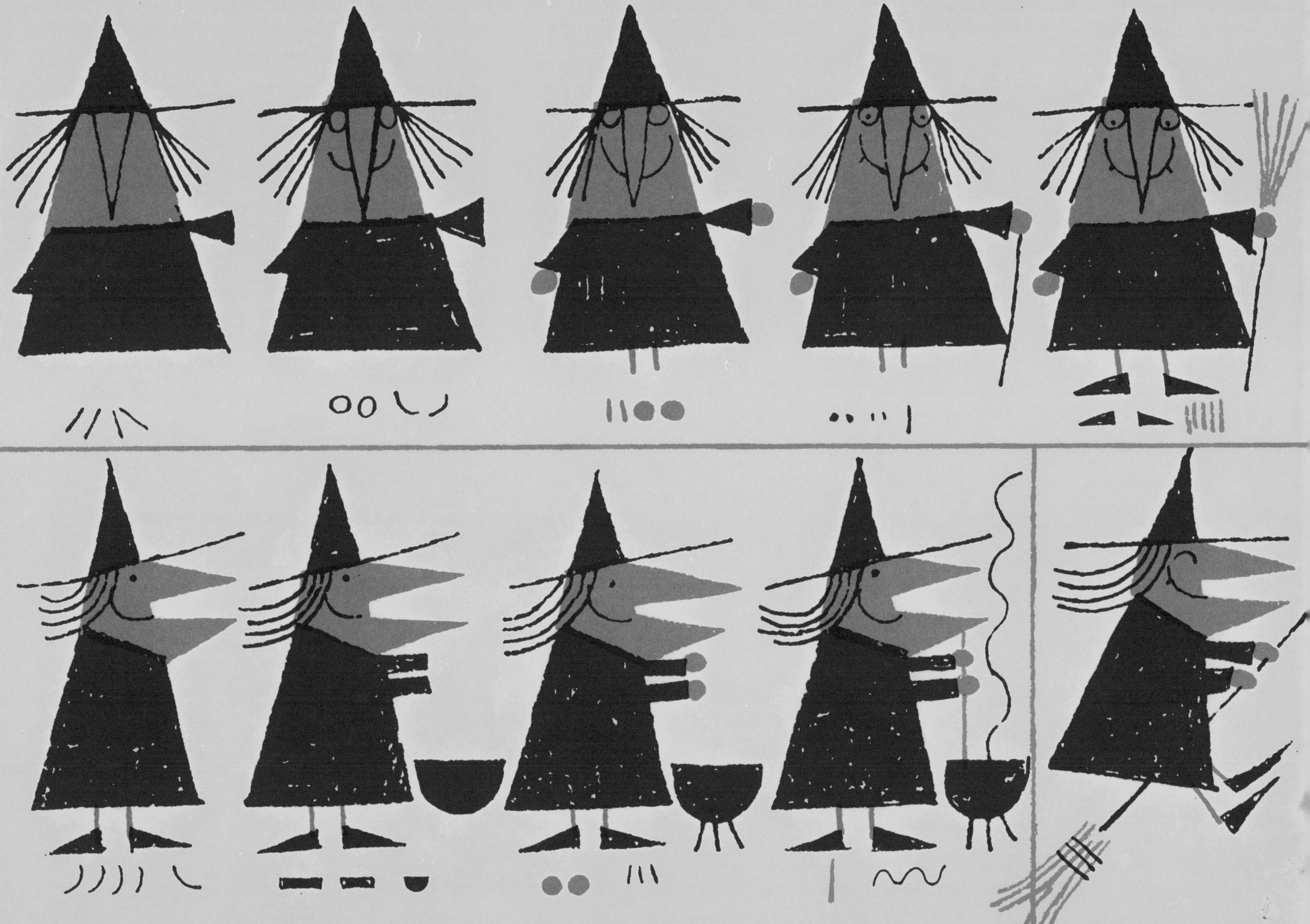

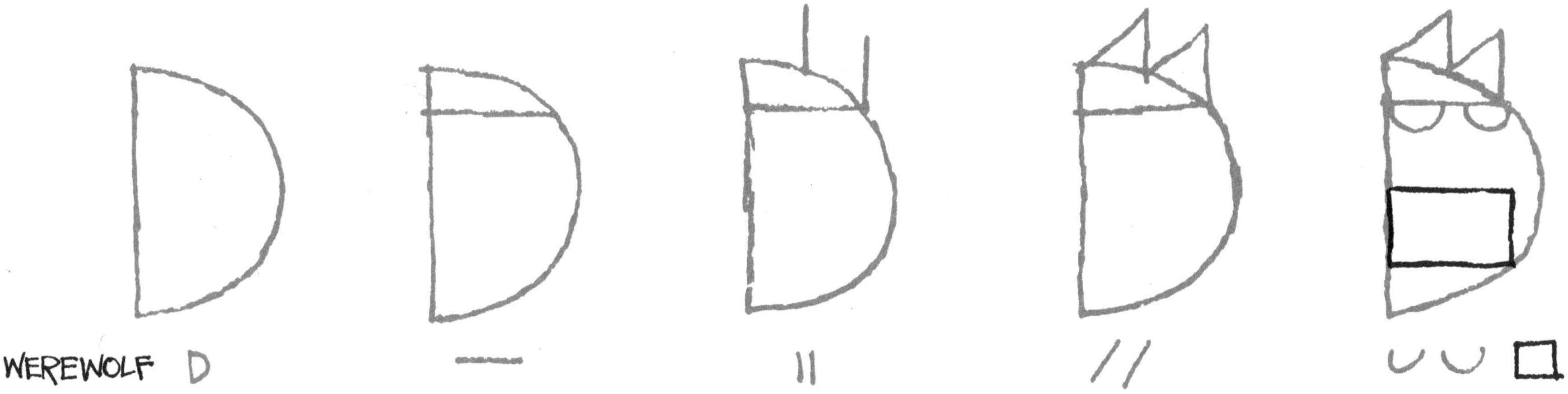
WEREWOLF

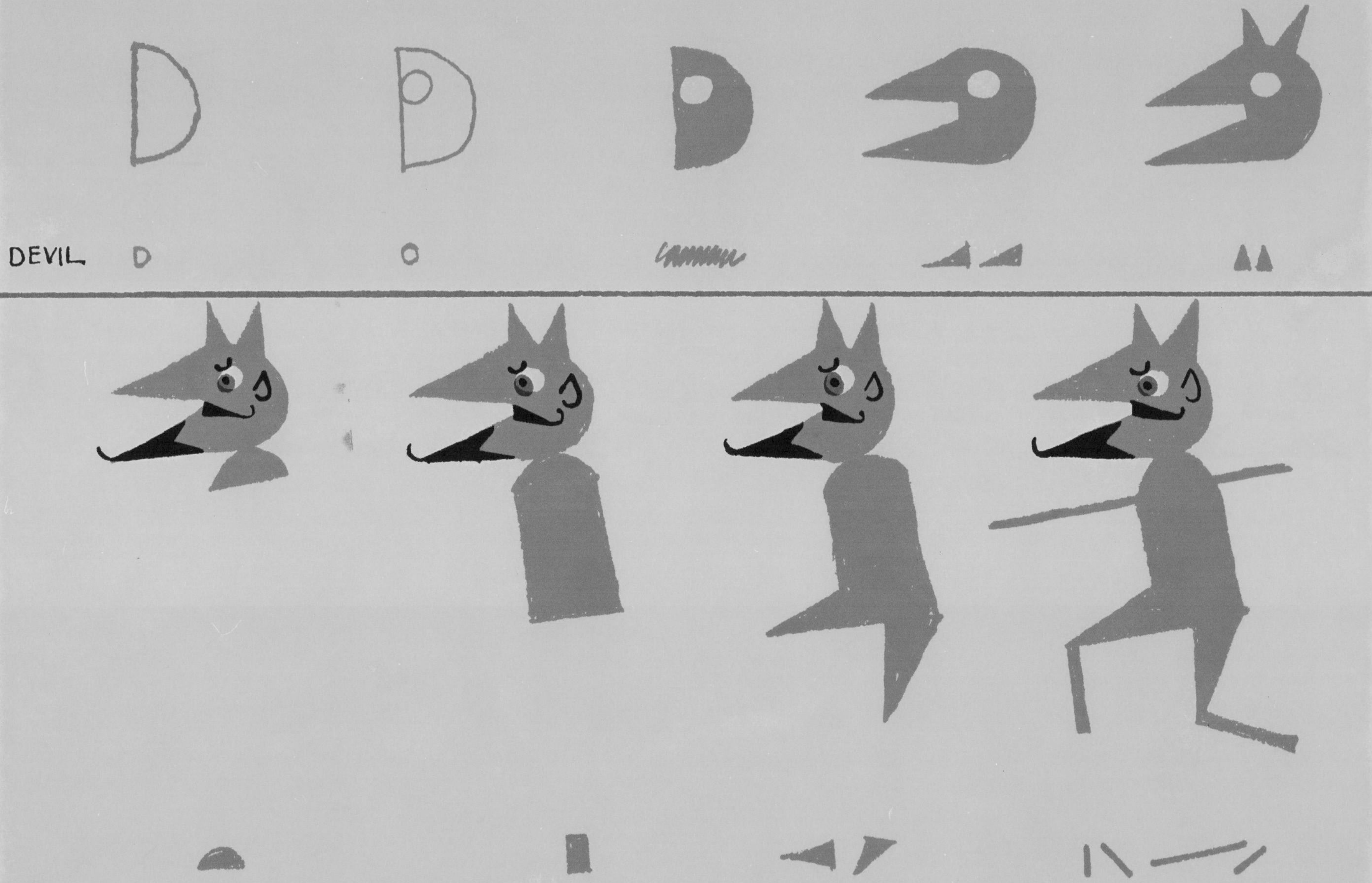
DEVIL

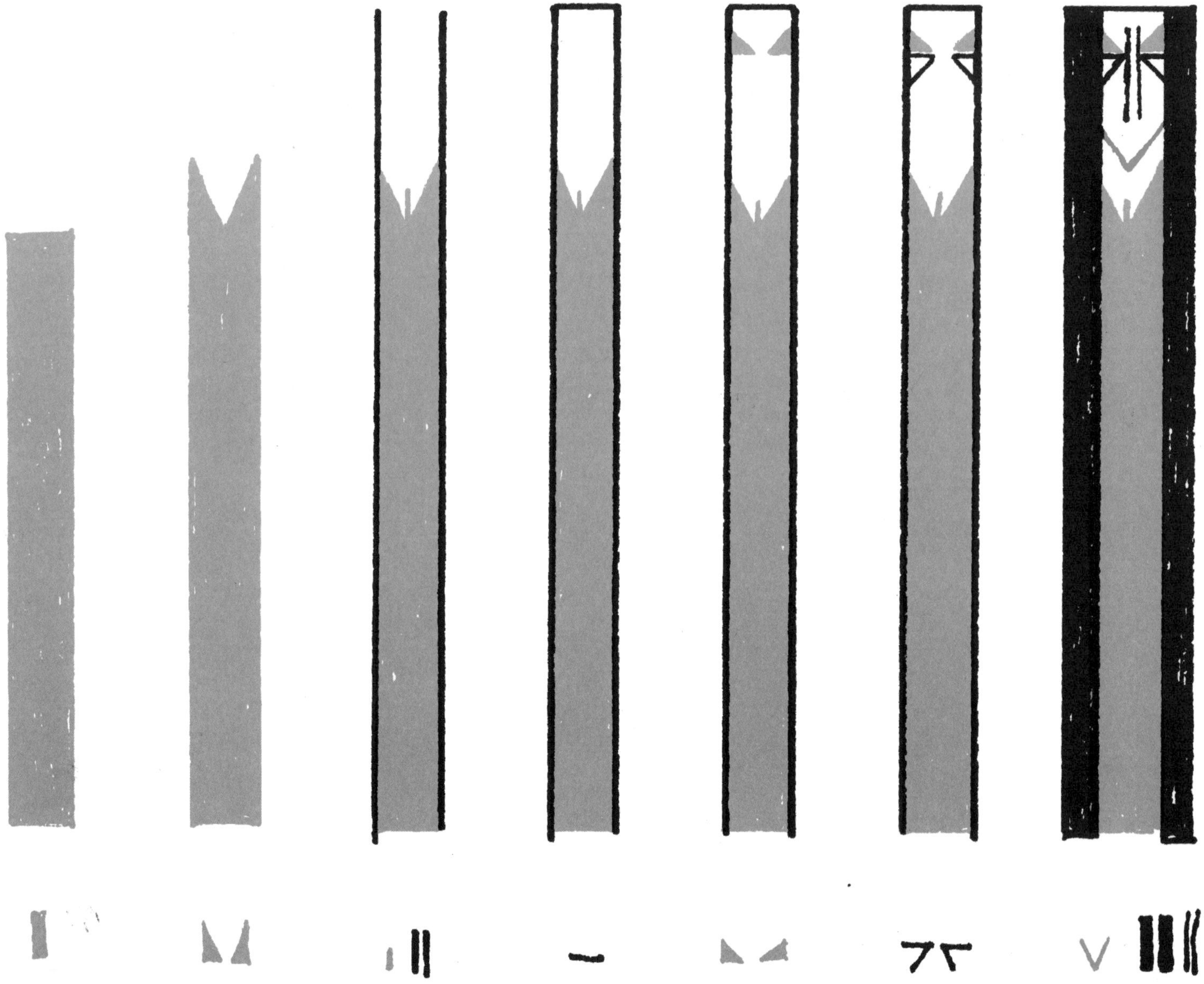

EVIL
EVA

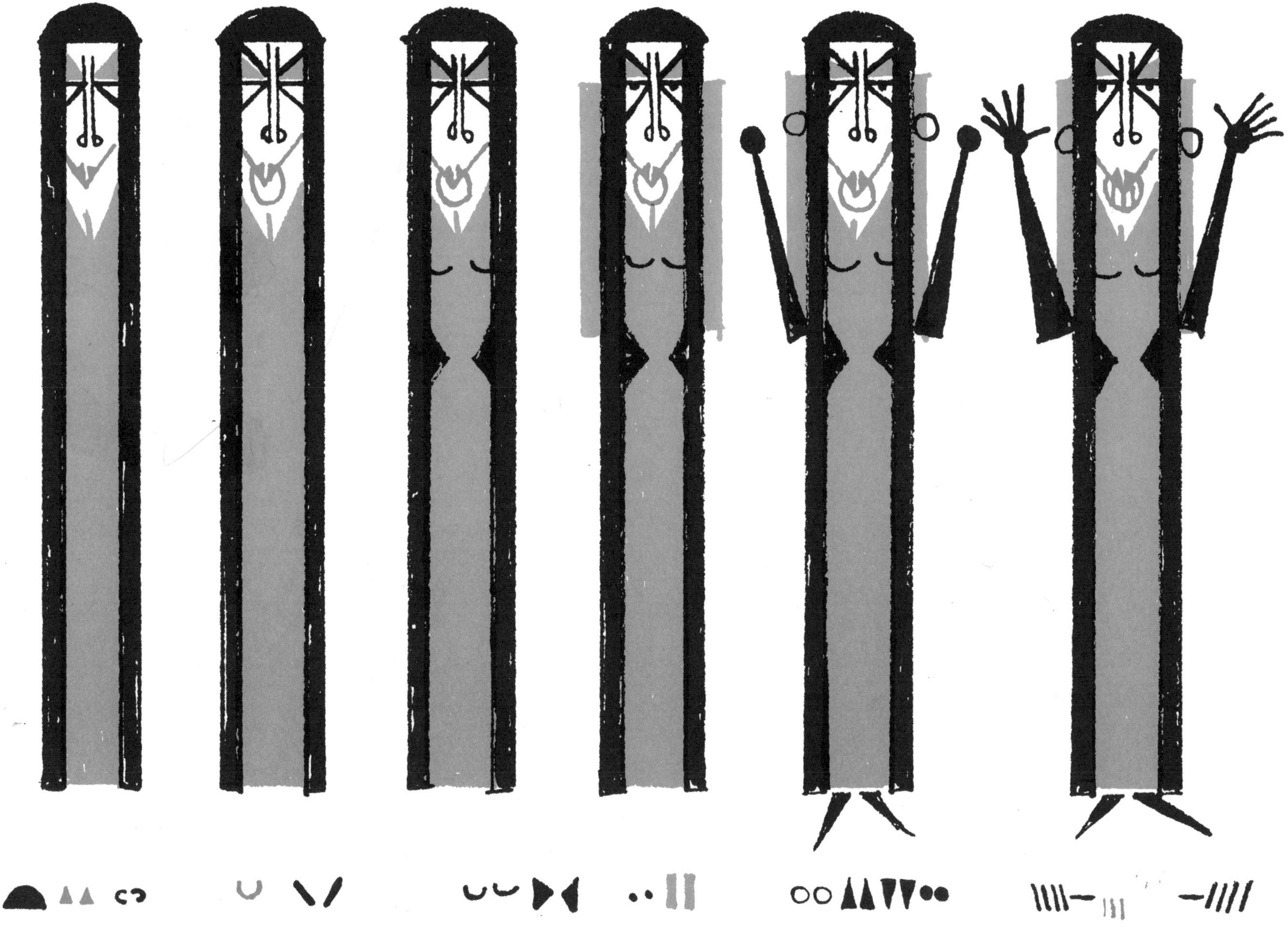

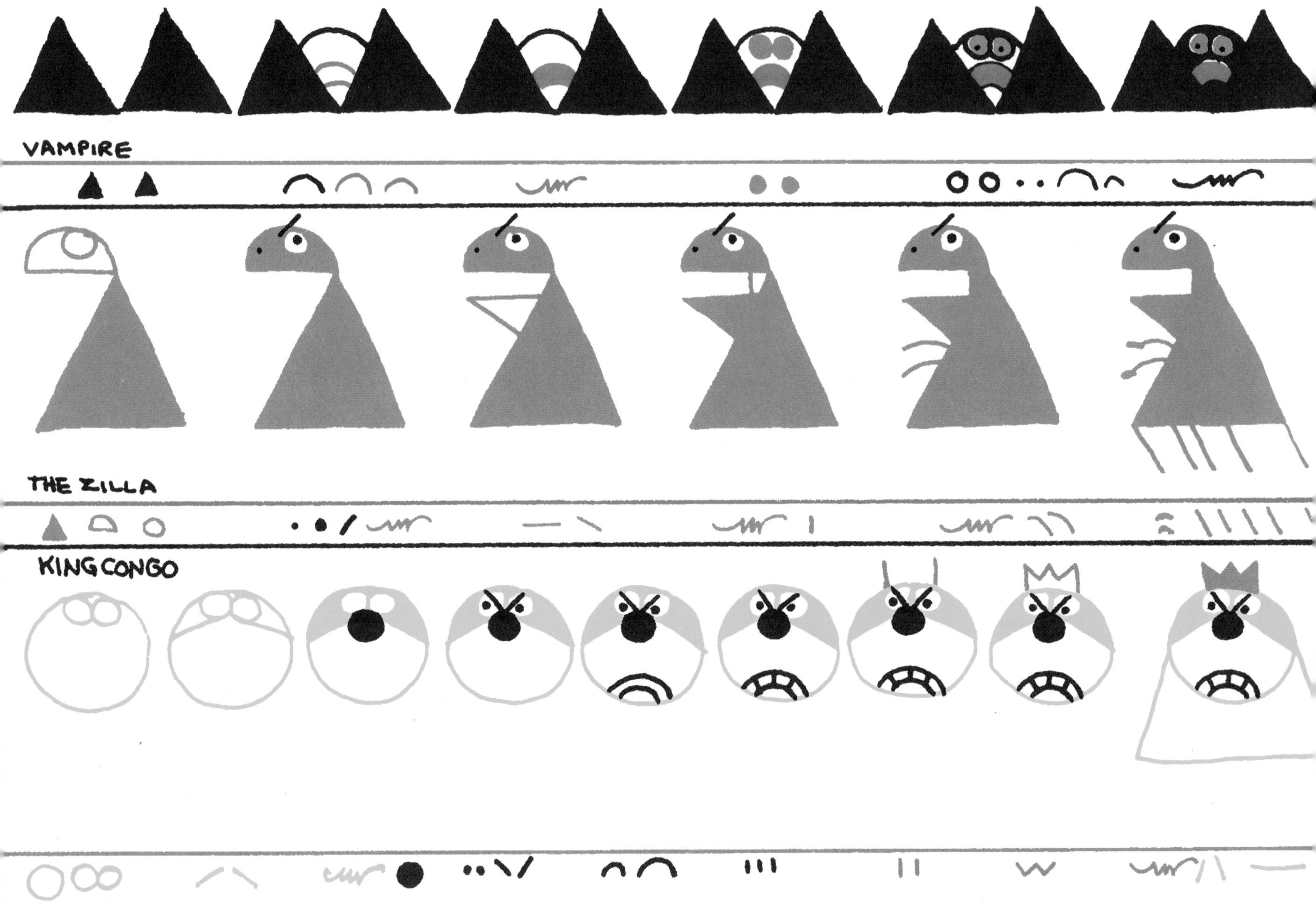
VAMPIRE
THE ZILLA
KINGCONGO

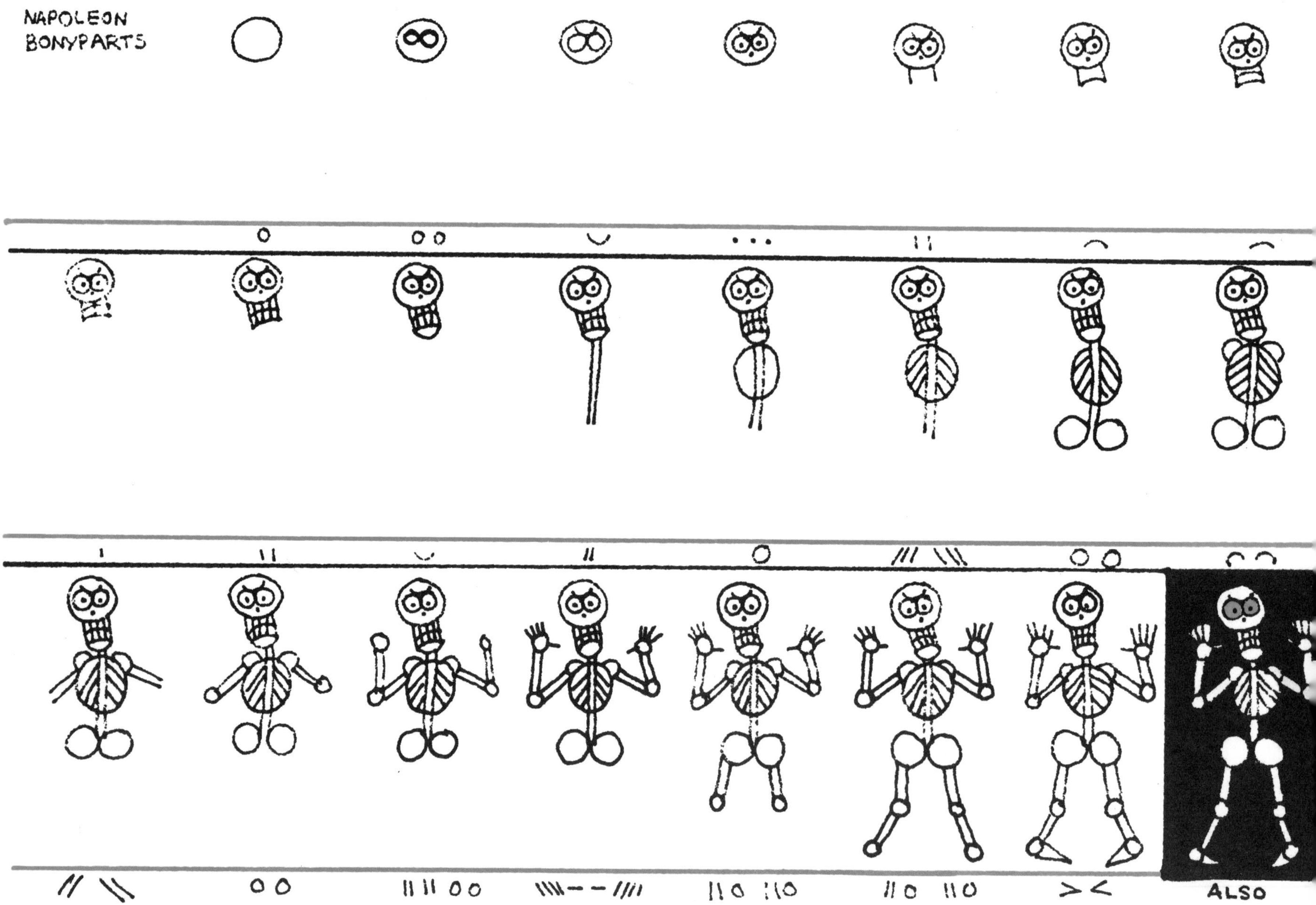
NAPOLEON
BONYPARTS
ALSO

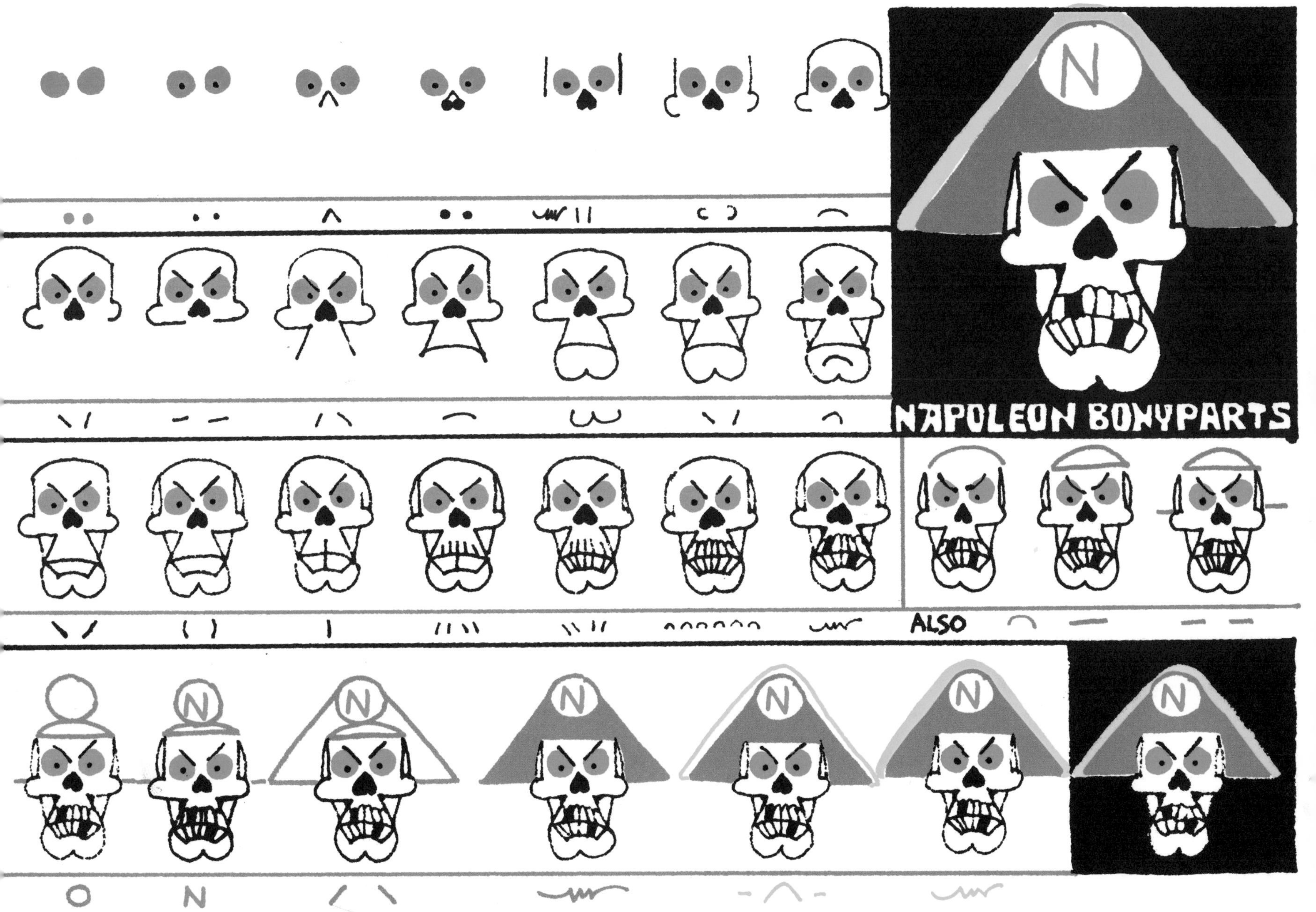

NAPOLEON BONYPARTS
ALSO
O
N

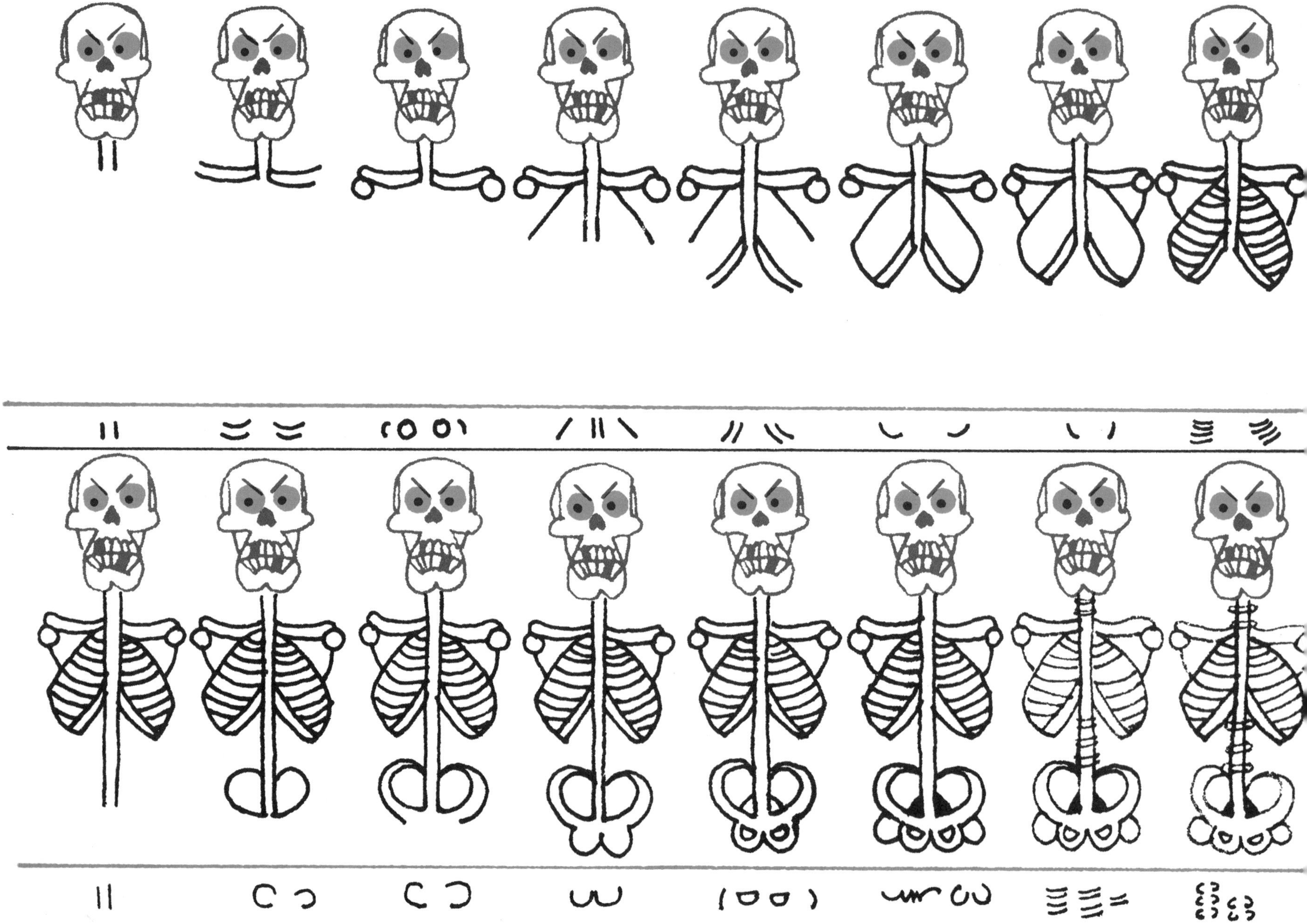

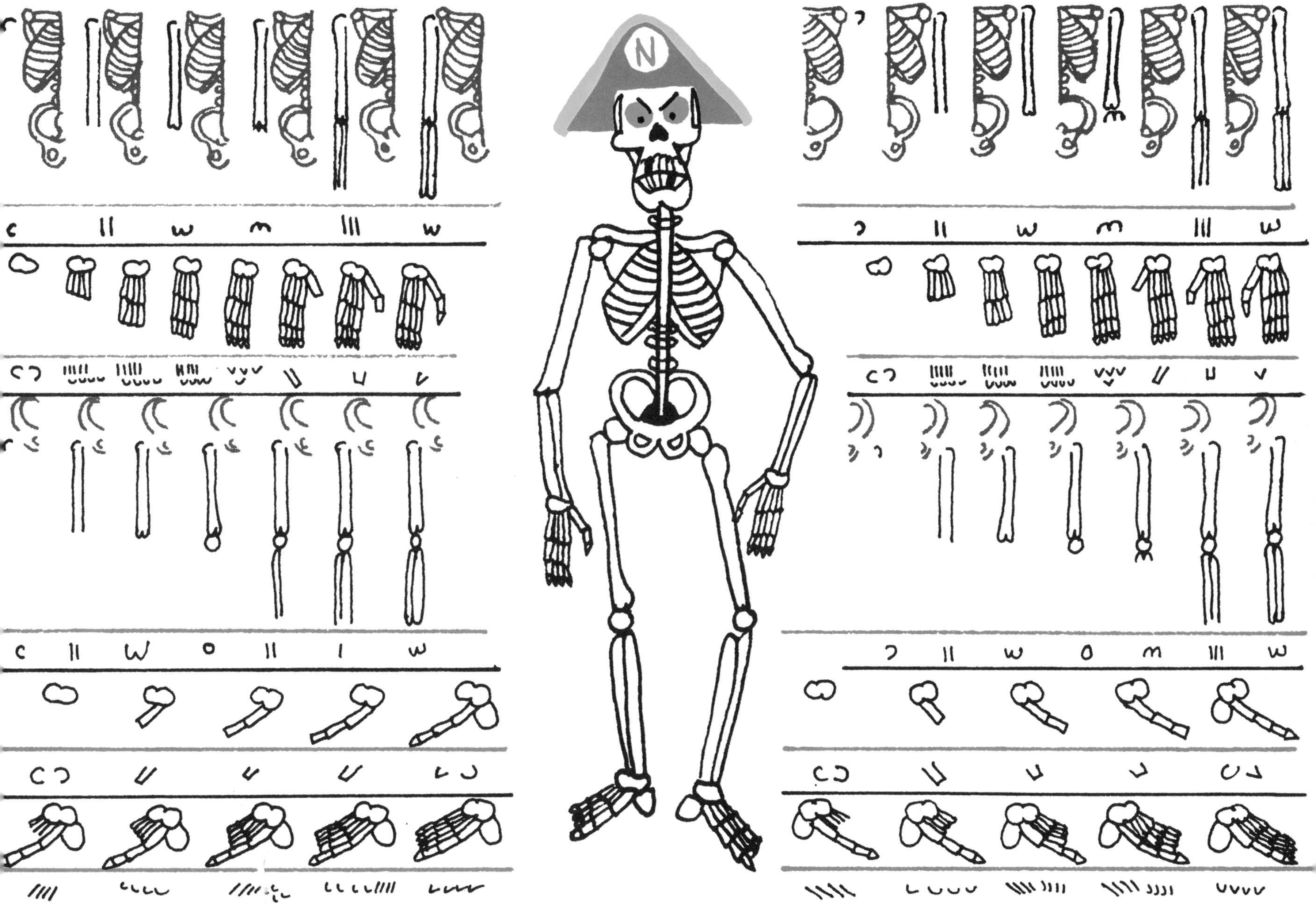

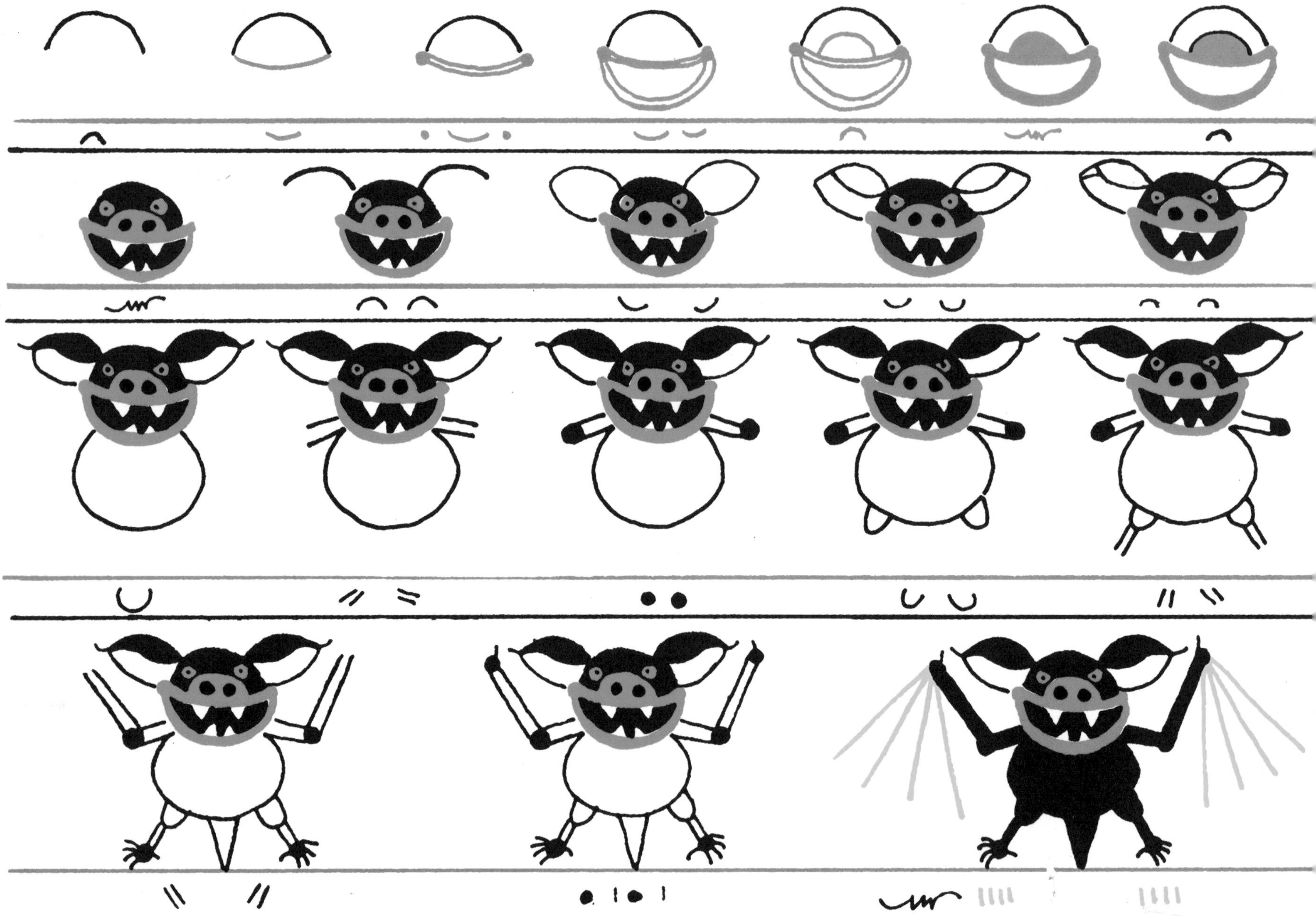

VAMPIRE
ALSO

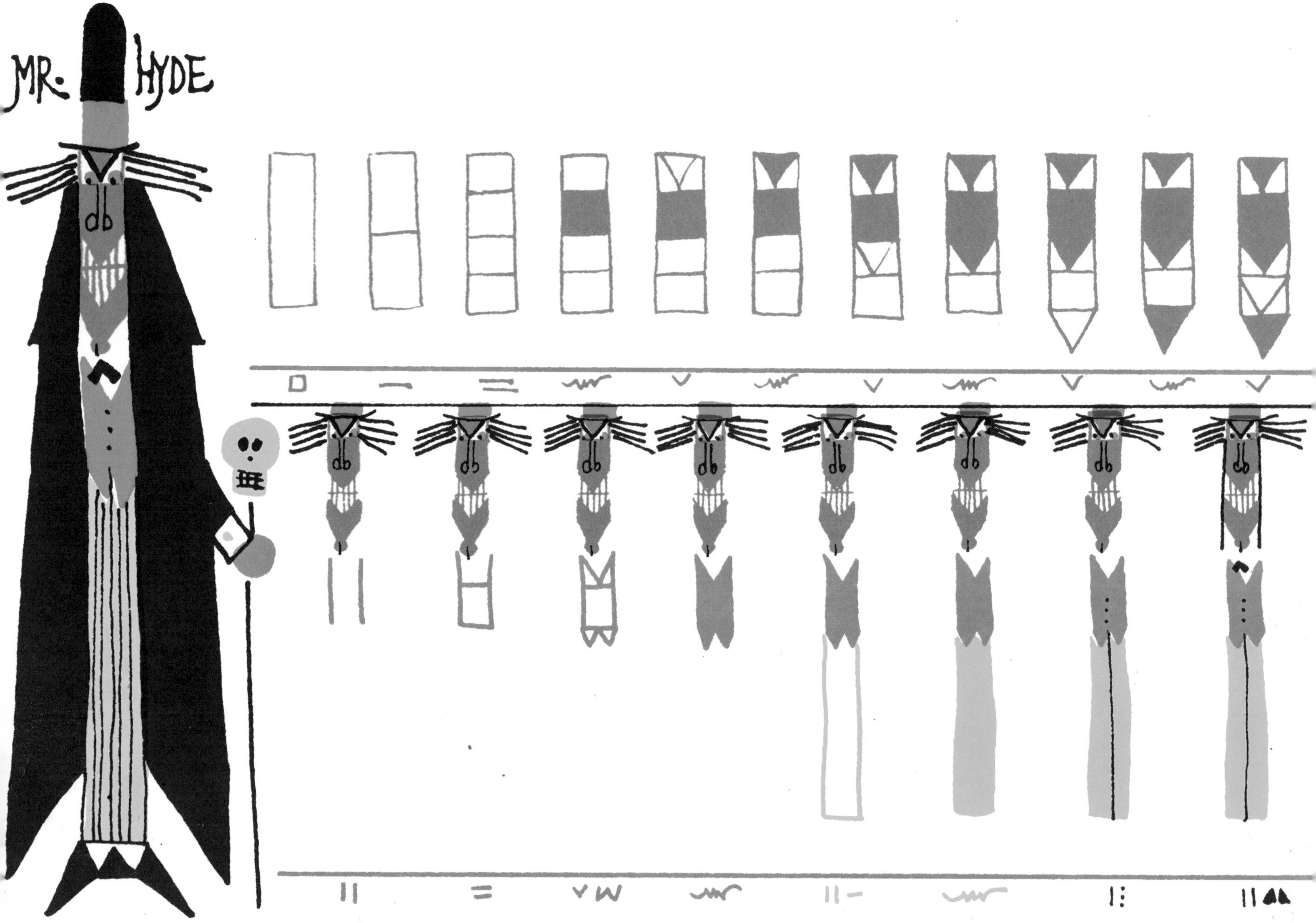
MR. HYDE

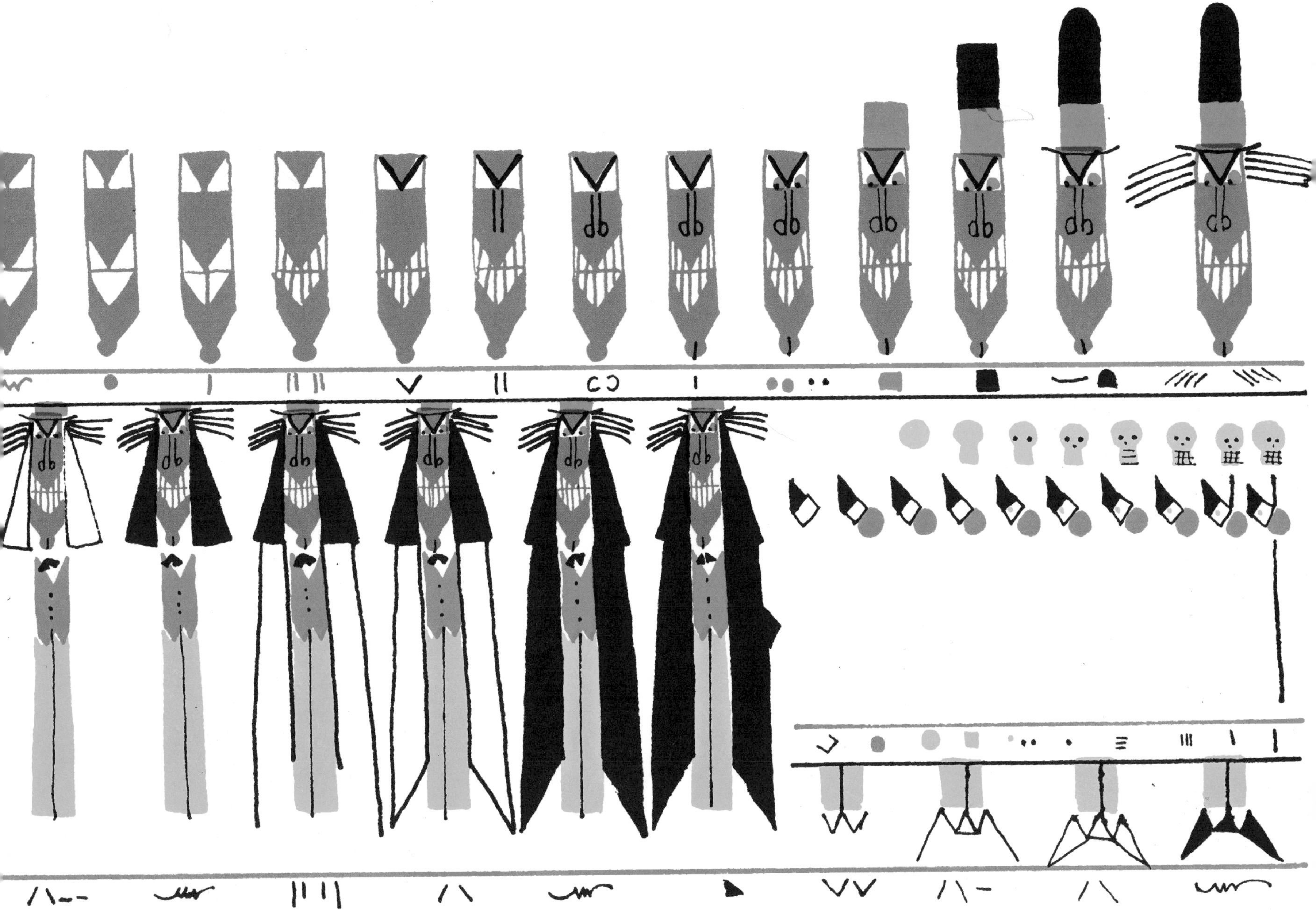

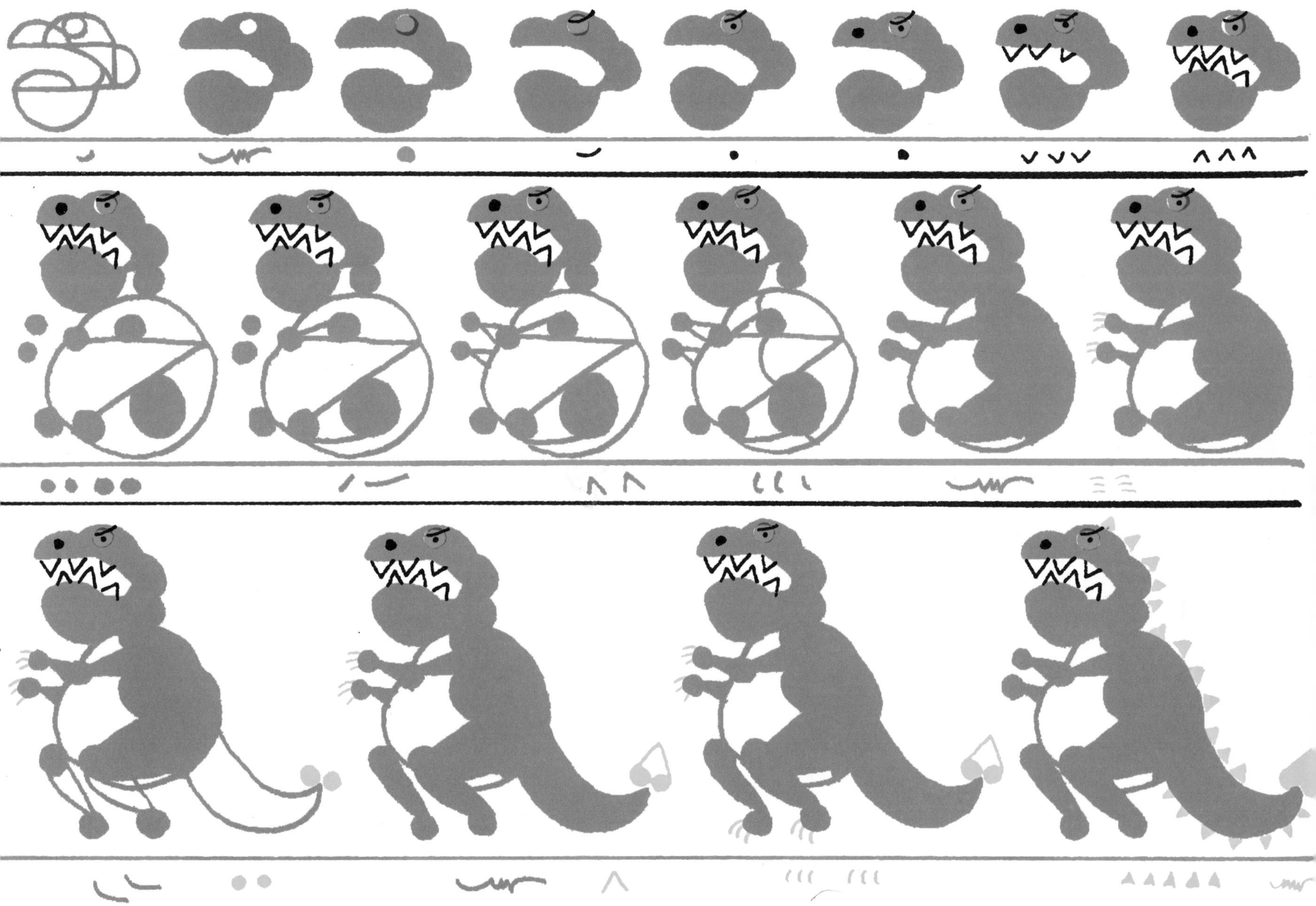

KING
CONGO

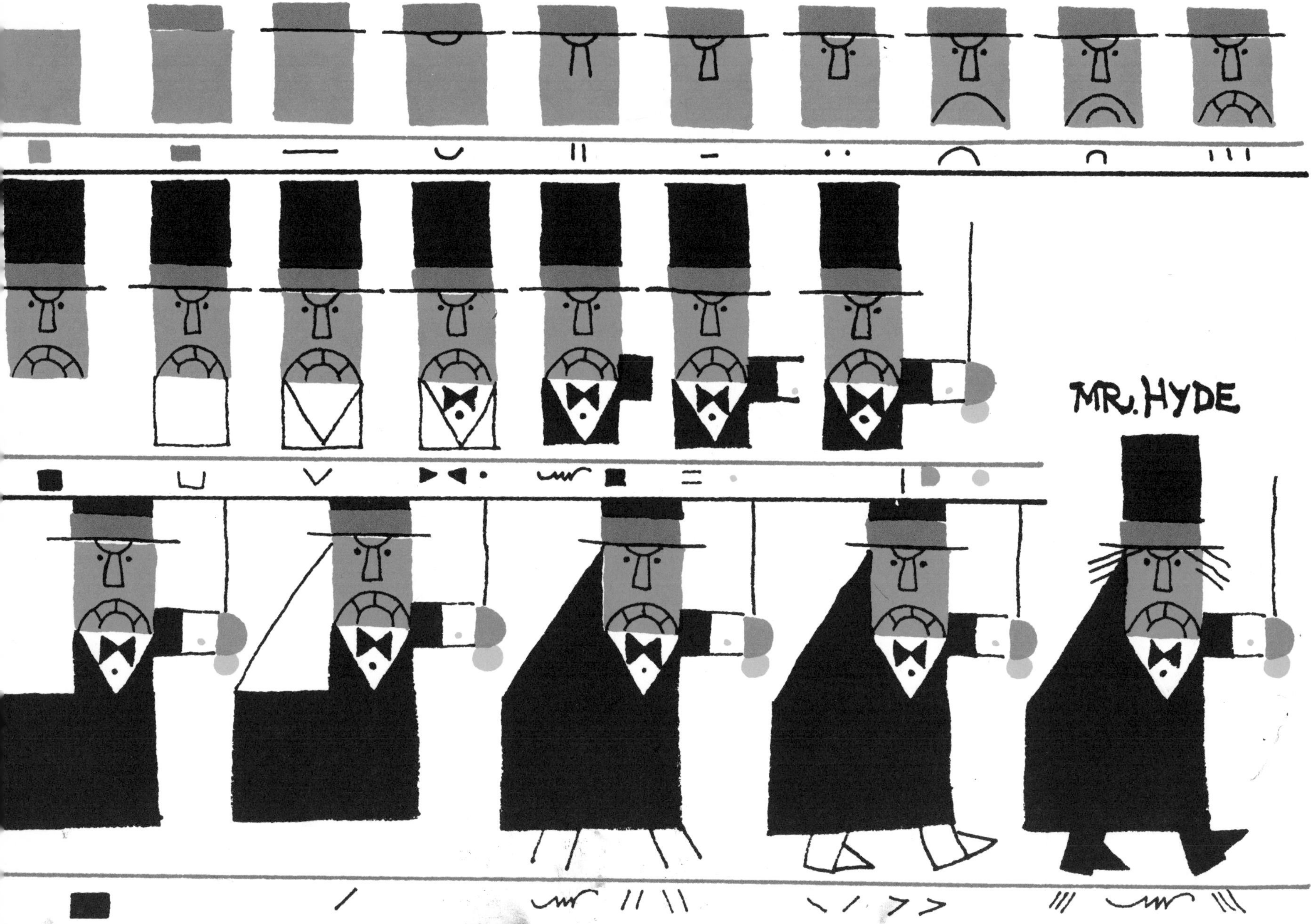
MR. HYDE

FOR MORE WEIRDOS, LOOK FOR:

Greengrin, Dr. Jekyll and Mr. Hyde, Frank, Dracula, and Dracula's Car in ED EMBERLEY'S BIG GREEN DRAWING BOOK.

Kreegor the Neebort, Ogre, Buttercup, and VampIrene in ED EMBERLEY'S BIG ORANGE DRAWING BOOK.

Swamp Creature in ED EMBERLEY'S BIG PURPLE DRAWING BOOK.

Bleezybub, Devil Dog, Foodle, and Feedle in ED EMBERLEY'S BIG RED DRAWING BOOK.

First Edition

ISBN 0-316-23546-6 (hc) / ISBN 0-316-23314-5 (pb)
LCCN 2001041385

10 9 8 7 6 5 4 3 2 1

Printed in Singapore